MW00889368

Forever Grateful To You:

Made in United States
Cleveland, OH
02 December 2024

11178899R00066